A NOTE TO PARENTS ABOUT OVERDOING IT

Moderation is not something that comes naturally to children. When left to their own devices, children often eat until they are sick, play until they are completely exhausted, and roughhouse until someone gets hurt.

The purpose of this book is to motivate children to "do all things in moderation." It is also to teach children how to relate to the people, places, and things in their lives in positive rather than negative ways.

Discussing this book with your child can help him or her get the most out of life without becoming indulgent and incurring unwanted side effects. It can also lay the foundation for later training regarding undesirable addictions such as the abuse of drugs and alcohol.

If ever there was a situation in which "actions speak louder than words," teaching a child about moderation is it. Teaching your child to avoid overindulgence while you are being indulgent will never work. In order to teach your child moderation, it is crucial that you practice it in every phase of your own life.

This book belongs to:

_____

Published by Scholastic Inc.
90 Old Sherman Turnpike, Danbury, CT 06816.

SCHOLASTIC and associated logos are trademarks and/or
registered trademarks of Scholastic Inc.

ISBN 0-7172-8575-8

First Scholastic Printing, October 2005

A Book About
Overdoing It

by
Joy Berry

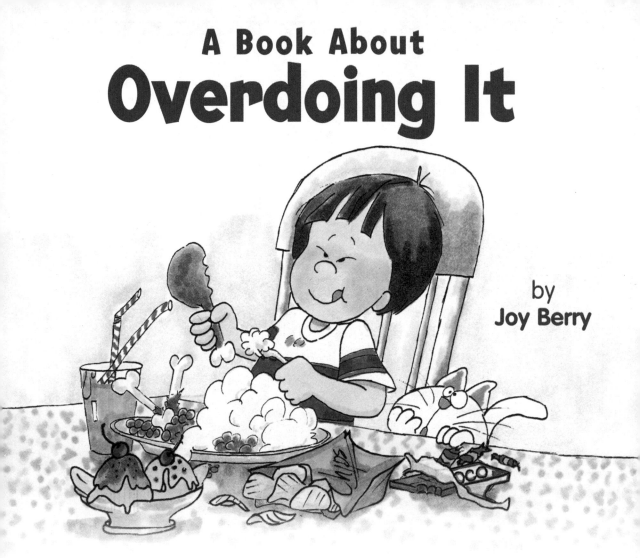

SCHOLASTIC INC.

New York   Toronto   London   Auckland   Sydney
Mexico City   New Delhi   Hong Kong   Buenos Aires

This book is about Lennie.

Reading about Lennie can help you understand and deal with **_overdoing it._**

You are overdoing it when you have too much of something. You are overdoing it when you do too much of something. Too much of anything can be harmful. When you overdo it, you can hurt yourself or others.

You can overdo it by *eating or drinking too much.* Try not to do this. Do these things instead:

- Take only a little bit of food at one time.
- Eat and drink slowly.
- Finish one mouthful of food before taking another.
- Do not eat so much that you feel stuffed.
- Do not eat too much of any one thing, especially sweets.

You can overdo it by *staying up too late* and *not getting enough sleep.*

Try not to stay up too late. Do these things instead:

- With your parent's approval, decide when you should go to bed.
- Give yourself at least half an hour before bedtime to get ready for bed.
- Go to bed on time. Do not put it off.

You can overdo it by *being around one person too much.*

Try not to be around any one person too much.

Have several playmates so that you will not have to play with one person all of the time.

Learn to play alone so that you can be by yourself when you need to be.

You can overdo it by *staying in one place too long.*

Try not to stay in any one place for too long.
Do these things instead:

- Go into another room if you have been in one room too long.
- Go outside if you have been inside too long.
- Go to a playground or to a friend's house if you have been at home too much.

You can overdo it by *doing something too much*. For example, you can overdo it by watching too much TV.

Try not to watch too much TV. Do these things instead:

- With the help of your parents, decide which TV programs you should watch.
- Turn on the TV only when it is time for one of these programs. Turn off the TV when the program is over.
- Try not to watch TV for more than one or two hours at a time.

You can overdo it by *being too rough.*

Try not to be rough with things. Do this instead:

- Find out how to use things properly.
- Use things the way they should be used.

You can overdo it by *playing too roughly with other people.* Playing too roughly can cause someone to get hurt. This is why you should avoid playing roughly with others.

It is important to not overdo it so you can enjoy the wonderful people, places, and things around you.